MINIMUM WAGE REVOLUTION

RICK MATSOKOTERE

ISBN: 978-1-9998765-9-3
Published By Green Cat Books

DEDICATION

For Elizabeth
You were the first to believe…..

CONTENTS

ACKNOWLEDGMENTS

To my mum, Perpetua Matsokotere. This book would have never been possible without your quiet hand of instruction, support and discipline over my life. I love you.

To my sister, Patronella, and my brother, Emmanuel, I hope I can be an inspiring big brother to you.

To the mentors I have had and in my life. First, Dr. Sunday Adelaja, the man whose words inspired me to get going and write this book. Steuart Payne, Mark Carter and Billy Lummis. Men among men.

To every manager, teacher and boss who shaped my attitude towards work. Liz Appleton, Mark Henning, Amanda Brown, Chris Preston, Julie Stone, Robert Batchelor, Steve Boddy and Gordon Hewitt. Thank you for giving me a chance to ply my craft.

And to everyone who has had the time to discuss and thrash out these ideas with me in thousands of hours of conversations. Thank you for being sounding boards to these concept.

INTRODUCTION

I was at the lowest point of my life. The bank was after me. Three different credit agencies were looking for where I was. I was sleeping on my mother's couch. The despair I felt gave me the first glimpse into the type of mental state a man could be in to contemplate suicide. My career, something I had previously took pride in, seemed like it had crashed and burned.

I needed to restart in a new city, with new friends and it was scary. I spent sleepless nights wondering where I was going to get the money and social capital to do something else at this stage of my life. I had reached career rock bottom and I had to muster up every single ounce of resolve and inner strength I had built over the years.

When my mind finally started to calm down, I began to see clearly what was ahead of me. After survival mode had kept me alive and I had settled my immediate concerns of sanity and basic provisions, I began to see the way forward. It was so simple that I wondered why I hadn't seen it before. You see, I had been here before and I had made something of myself from nothing.

When I started my career, I had one of the worst jobs according to societal standards. I worked at McDonalds. However, I had been resourceful and pulled myself to a much better job and career with one of the top companies in the UK. I had even inspired other young men and women to boost their own careers through my story and advice, but now it was me who needed to drink my own cool-aid!

I found myself in the age-old philosophical conundrum, "If I could start again knowing what I know now, what would I do differently?" I was wiser, I was more focused and more importantly, I had a lot more at stake as I started working an entry level position.

If you take the action I suggest with each of the principles put forward in this book, you can take control of your job, your career and your life. No longer will you think that the minimum wage, low wage or entry level job that you are in or looking to get, is trivial. You will find the joy of working with purpose and direction, knowing where you could go with it to find the most fulfilment in your work.

This book is about the true meaning of work compared to a job, it is about making the best lemonade from the lemons of a minimum wage job and it is about getting out of poverty and despair. I will walk you through the different directions in which you can go from the bottom of the career ladder to the pinnacle of what is important to you. It will be practical and it will be specific, so get ready to take action, just like I have.

With love, Rick Matsokotere

PROLOGUE

This book is meant to be as practical as it is informative. The knowledge contained within its pages are not meant to be read and then ignored, but they are intended to challenge you to take your life into your own hands. The book, therefore, is written in a simple way that structures the main points and concepts into clearly defined parts and chapters. Each chapter has a separate idea that is intended to be able to stand on its own merit.

I have found most readers of non-fiction books tend to read in this way, taking it all one chapter at a time, so you can take your time studying each chapter, which will lead naturally into the next.

To get the most out of the book:

1. Make notes, mind maps and mark the book if you need to. It is your book and I would rather have you get something out of it than have it look pretty.

2. Either start each chapter or end it by going over the golden nuggets that can be found at the conclusion of the chapter. These are a concise summary of the main ideas of what was discussed in that chapter.

3. Try out the practical tips that are provided at your job today! Have fun with it and see it work for you.

RICK MATSOKOTERE

PART 1 – LOW WAGE WORK

"I want to create an economy where minimum wage is a very brief stepping stone to higher-paying jobs so people can realize their dreams."

Thom Tillis – Senator for North Carolina

CHAPTER 1 – WORKING A LOW WAGE JOB

On at least four occasions in my working life, I have found myself in low wage or at least entry level positions in companies I worked for. The first couple of times I didn't know what I was getting into, but on the third rodeo, I knew I had something tremendous in my hands. Many people who find themselves at the point of having a low wage job, maybe you, may be asking, "So what do I do now?"

So, you don't have the big bucks! So, you may not be looked upon as the top of the social ladder by your friends and family. I believe, however, that there are so many possibilities, opportunities and doors available to you in this situation.

Working a minimum wage job is not the end of your life. Whether you are just starting at Subway after college or university, or you are having to start as a brick layer after a couple of years out of work, or if you are starting over as an office administrator after your previous career didn't work out. Agreed, prospects may not be the best for you and at times you may feel taken advantage of and undervalued in this level of work, but you can use a minimum wage job as a starting point for a new career and a new outlook for life. The good thing about starting at the bottom of a ladder is that you can go anywhere you want!

FINDING HOPE

There really is hope for you out there, just as there was hope for me and there has been hope for many men and women who have made the most of themselves from the same gloomy starting point as you may feel you are in right now. There are possibilities that are open. Beginning at the bottom means there is nowhere to go but up for you. You may not see a way out of the boredom and banality of the low wage work you are in but there is light at the end of that tunnel, that is what I want to highlight to you with this book.

It is the same as a fallen tree I saw once next to a stream in a nature reserve in Portsmouth. The tree itself looked as if it was dead and gone, but on closer inspection, near the stream, were shoots that were starting to come out of the trunk. It reminded me of a section of a poem that I heard once,

"There is hope for a tree, even though it be cut down. Yet at the scent of water, it will burst forth again."

Anonymous

Hope is a much-needed thing in our 21st century world. Hope keeps us alive, it makes us human and it makes life worth living. The reason we don't all simply commit suicide is that we have hope. So look at working a minimum wage job with hope for what can be. You, at least, have a little something in your hand in the form of that job, that you can take and make great. You may not have a big stake in the world economy or the way your city and country is run, but your menial job is something.

COUNT YOUR ADVANTAGES

When starting a low wage job, you have something. Let's count what you do have.

When you have a low wage job, what is it that you have in your hand? Firstly, you now have a foot on the career ladder. If you are working in a small business, you have the chance to help the founder and builder of that business to grow his or her enterprise into something big. If like me, you enjoy working for big companies, then you have a foothold in a corporation with opportunities for internal promotion, pay rises and upskilling. As long as you look for chances, you can have access to internal vacancies, trainee positions within your company, and the like.

It is possible to get promoted if you work for it. In chapter 2 I will really give you some nuts and bolts about how to make this happen deliberately. For now, though, I will remind you that many people have gone from coming into a company at the bottom and worked their way to the top.

Secondly, you now have some money. If you were unemployed or in school before this job, then chances are you had nothing of your own. You simply were at the mercy of those who were helping you. While on benefits, this is the case that the government is helping you to get back on your feet. You, however, have no wealth of your own. You may think they are "your" benefits but all it takes is a radical change in political winds for you to realise you own nothing. With a minimum wage job, at least you will have some money of your own. This is something you can count in the win column of your finances and life.

You can buy your basic essentials and live on your own terms. You no longer have to borrow or go deep in debt just for your family to eat. You can pay off your loans and get the bailiffs off your back. You can restore your dignity by being able to fend for yourself and contribute to household needs. You don't need to rely on your partner for the most basic little things.

Thirdly, you have to realise you still have your talents, gifts and skills. These are those assets you were either born with or that you acquired in life. Just because you had to get a low wage job, it doesn't mean that those things that you were born with that make you peculiar and special, have been stripped from you. If you happen to be stacking shelves on the night shift, you still have your skills. If you happen to be flipping burgers, your personality is still something you have going for you. You need to count these advantages that you have every day.

Now, you must use these talents and gifts periodically, because just like any other muscle, if left unused for a period they can atrophy and waste away. But it is in you. Find a way to remind yourself of the talents that are inside you, then find a way to practice them and make them better, not worse, while you work a low wage job.

Let's say you have a great intellectual mind and enjoy learning and studying, but you are working in an elderly home, caring for and assisting residents. If you use that as an excuse to never pick up a book again then that is your own fault. Your intellectual talent will not be taken from you, but if you neglect it, you may forget how to use it well. If you pick it up again later, it will take a while to get back into the swing of things.

Let me tell you a little bit of what happened to me. As a 19-year old I joined McDonalds and quickly got into a culture of going out clubbing after each payday. When I finally rediscovered reading with personal development materials 4 years later, I could not get back to my nerd levels straight away, but I started to build the habit again. I had to pull on this studious habit in 2016, when I found myself in a bad place. After losing my first business and ending up on my mother's sofa, I found myself in a new city with no relationships, no money but lots of debt.

I first tended to my emotional health which was the most important thing, then I set about assessing what I still had. The thing I had, I finally realised, was my story. 12 years prior, I had started at McDonalds then worked myself to become a manager. I had done this at 23, but now I was older and wiser. I happened to be more knowledgeable now, was more focused and knew that what took 4 years the first time, I could do in a year if I wanted to. When my local petrol station advertised a night shift job, I saw my opportunity to work, make some decent money and have my daytime hours to build my new business as a writer. It was with this understanding that I began to look at the glass of my life as half full and began to work for BP.

My plan was to work for a couple of years in this job whilst building a business as an author and ghost writer, using my small wage as starting capital to get myself off the ground without getting into debt. If all went to plan, I was to build my small business to the point where it made much more money than I was making in my low wage job. I would be doing my best in my new job even though I was not planning on getting any promotion whilst there. To satisfy my own need to do well

I decided to work so smart and hard that I would be recognised as the best worker in that shop. I would support my manager so much that he would have no choice but to recognise me as his most valuable employee. Doing this, I felt, would boost my confidence in my ability after the business failure and allow me to prove again that the principles that I am talking about will work for anyone in any place.

YOU CANNOT KEEP A GOOD MAN DOWN

I admit, working a low wage or entry level job can be demoralising. Perhaps it's that the job is mundane, it's hard on your body, it's mind-numbing or it's looked down upon by your peers. After all, if every time you meet your mates after a hard day at the job you smell like fried chicken from your KFC gig, then they may mention it in jest a few times. There is a temptation to lose hope that you could ever get out of this position. You could lose your self-confidence and start to doubt your very purpose in life as well as your dreams. However, I would like to suggest you not lose hope. I have learnt that, in life, you cannot keep a good man down.

How can I assert that you can't keep a good man down? Even in a job at the bottom of the food chain, the good things that make you valuable cannot be suppressed. In fact, those assets that you have inside you will cause you to rise to success in some of the most unlikely of places. Like a flower, your strengths will blossom and cause you to be noticed by the decision makers if you shine a light of focus on them.

Take Joshua for instance. He was always intelligent and wanted to study Quantity Surveying in one of the top universities in London. Unfortunately, it didn't work out for him to attend because his grades were not good enough to enter his choices of universities.

What Joshua did, however, was think outside the box. He went to a South African university for two years then got an internship to do the rest of his studies being sponsored by Network Rail. In the end, the education he got was considerably cheaper and he got experience that propelled him ahead of his peers. All from an unfortunate circumstance that happened, which he didn't let get him down. He could have given up and doubted the intelligence that his family and teachers had always affirmed in him, but instead he chose to keep going, knowing his talent would show in the end.

There are many people who feel beat down by having a job that seems like it is a dead end. This drives many people into depression, mental health issues, drug use and even crime. All this happens when people lose hope and this is why hope is important.

Consider that when you were a child, you had an optimistic view of life. Somewhere along the line, as you grew up, this may have been taken away from you, but my goal with this book is to assure you that the real you, the you that is good, can be encouraged to rise to the surface. Your job, despite what it may have seemed like so far, can be a vehicle for this to happen. Don't let your low wage job kill your inner man or woman, but use your job as a stepping stone to becoming great. You can dream again. You will have to do some mental work and you will have to become better than you are currently, but this is what is necessary to becoming the person of your dreams.

EVERYTHING AND EVERYONE HAS TO START SOMEWHERE

The fact that things start as seeds and then grow is a universal one. It is a law of life on planet earth. The truth of seed, time and harvest means that every plant starts with a seed then with time, becomes a harvest. In the same way, all things start small then become big. You start with a single object, then it multiplies to become many.

Every biological life form starts in seed form. It is provable scientific fact. Every plant and animal on earth starts as a seed. Whether it is a plant seed, a sperm, an egg, it all starts as an embryo then grows and germinates to become the grown species. There are no exceptions. First is seed level, then infancy followed by adulthood. Following this principle, your career also has to start somewhere.

This is where the change of paradigm needs to happen. A paradigm is a world view you may hold since childhood. Are you in a crappy job? Or are you simply starting a great career journey? As you look at your minimum wage job, can you look at it a bit differently? There is always new perspective that can be found in life.

Three men were laying bricks one day. Asked to describe what they were doing, one said, "I'm laying some bricks." The second said, "I'm building a wall." The third said, "I'm helping to build a shopping mall that will be a hub of entertainment in our city!" Consider the difference in perspective among these people. The first and second could not see past the task at hand. The second guy was a bit better but he could not see past the brick wall. The third man had a bigger vision. Yes, he was engaged in a mundane task, but he knew the greater significance and greater plan.

Do you have the outlook of man 1, 2 or 3 from the story? Every person who ever got to the top of their field started somewhere. Many of the managers at the pinnacle of large organisations started at the bottom.

Consider Horst Schulze. For many years he was the President of the Ritz Carlton hotel chain. He is considered to have changed the way luxury hotels operate and is a pioneer of the modern-day guest experience at the top hotels of the world. Horst credits the insight and genius he has to the many menial jobs that he started out doing in the hotel industry. He made beds, worked in kitchens, carried bags, cleaned carpets all the way up until he was running the hotel chain. To this day, Horst never forgets his roots, talking with empathy as he inspires his maids and bell hops in each hotel. He appreciates them because he did the exact same jobs as they are now doing. It was the diligence in customer service that took him to the top and now he earns millions of dollars for his trouble. Remember that word DILIGENCE as we are going to revisit it later in the book.

So, are you just starting on your journey to greatness? Your journey can take many directions. It could be that you start in a low wage job then get to the point you are promoted to become a leader and manager. Many people have ended up in CEO positions through this process being repeated over and over again. You may not be a leader in the conventional management roles of most companies, but you could have talents and skills that are valuable in their own right. Other people have started in entry level positions and pivoted to go into the IT or accounting department of their company. These people can rise to become engineers, head chefs, administrators and trainers in the end. The difference with them is that they followed what they were interested in, not just the management position that came with higher pay. You can move laterally within your company.

WHERE YOU GO FROM HERE IS YOUR CHOICE

I have discovered, after considering the lives of over a thousand of the most successful people in human history then comparing to the lives of us ordinary folks, that you can be poor, middle class or rich. It all depends on what you choose to do with the little you were given.

The vast majority of readers of this book will probably be in the poor class. If you are in a minimum wage or low wage job, then you are working class. Unfortunately, when it comes to opportunities for your children, where you end up living or chances to live great experiences, this is not the best class to be in. I urge you to follow that natural desire to rise up in your station in life.

Are you, like most people whether they admit to it or not, striving to go from low to middle class? The principles laid out in this book will definitely help you to do that. Personally, I'm convinced it is better to be in the class of the rich. This is where true independence is and as you will see, I am not a fan of being a slave of any world system. I am, however, empathetic of the fact that most readers have not thought about what I am introducing, whilst I have had over a decade to think these things through. The book, then, will also help you to take your initial steps.

In conclusion, this first chapter, meant to serve as a reminder that you have a little something in your life, even it be a low-level job in the eyes of the world. In the next chapter, I will point to your true worth, both intrinsically and when it comes to net worth.

THE GOLDEN NUGGETS

1. There is hope for you even if you are working the worst job – at least you have something.

2. Your job is a tool you have in your hand which can be turned into a career.

3. If you are a hard worker and a good person, you cannot be kept down in a dead-end job.

4. Like every life form begins in seed form, so will any career you will have in life. Your job is simply that starting point.

RICK MATSOKOTERE

CHAPTER 2 – KNOW YOUR WORTH

In the last chapter, we talked about what you have when you are working a low wage job. In this one, I will press to you the importance of understanding yourself and what you are worth, despite your job.

YOUR WORTH AS A HUMAN BEING

Work is very important to us humans. With all people, you will see that work is crucial to us. We find out that we are placed on earth to accomplish certain things and this is what we end up conflating with our jobs. Jobs are bludgeoned into us all through school and culture so that one can grow up believing that his job and his life's work is the same thing.

This, however, is not the case! In fact, I would like to compare and contrast the two; WORK vs a job. You can agree that a job and work have become interchangeable words in modern vocabulary. I purposefully have used them in this way in the book to prove my point.

A job is a role that fits into the system of this world we live in that takes your time, then rewards you with some money, with the goal being to meet the ends of that system. Your work, however, is what you are on earth to do. It is something specific to you, making use of your highest talents and most intrinsic values to bring out a result that is pure and beneficial to humankind.

You must not confuse and conflate your work and your job. This is important because working a job has been beat down into us in the western world to such an extent that it consumes almost everything we do. As a result, if we confuse these two things, our roles can become entwined with who we think we are, and our mental picture of who we are as people. If you are mother, this could be applied to raising your children. You can lose a grip on who you are as an individual because of your role. You could start to believe that taking care of those kids you love so much is the only reason you are alive. What happens, then, for example, if the children decide to live on their own or if they die? I will expand on why you must not live in this way as we go on with this chapter.

WHO DEFINES YOU?

The first question to ask yourself is, "Who defines my intrinsic worth?" If you do not come to grips with what you are worth as a human being, you could be led to look at what you get paid, your job title or how people respond to your job status for validation of your worth. This is an extremely dangerous way to look at things. Let's say you are a waiter in a restaurant and all your friends look at you as if you're nothing because of that job.

It's totally possible to go around thinking that even after you walk out of the restaurant and take off your apron, you are still beneath the people around you. Perhaps you believe you are worth less than the patrons you served because of the way they speak to you every day.

I beg to differ! You are the only person who is qualified to define what you are worth. You are not defined by your manager or the people who look down at you. You have to say to yourself, "I am who I am!" Then go ahead to redefine yourself.

Here's a pointer as to how to define yourself in a healthier way. First, you are a human being. Just that fact means that you are worth a lot. Human rights are all the proof you need. If you consider that the world has placed value on human life, this should be enough to give you permission to redefine yourself, just in case I wasn't enough authority for you. You are alive in the 21st century and you are a living human being. The combined worth of the living machine that is your body will stagger you. You have a mind, a heart and an intangible personality. You can love, you can speak and you can articulate yourself. Even if you are physically disabled, you have value in your other working faculties. You should feel proud and happy to be alive to read this.

T. Harv Eker, the author of the bestseller, Secrets Of The Millionaire Mind, tells the story of how he worked at an ice cream parlour while he was working on ideas of the business he was going to start. He needed to know how ice cream shops worked so that he could later on source and sell the equipment needed by the stores. Harv knew what he was worth, so that even though he worked at that place, he did not get dragged into feeling depressed that he was making and selling ice cream every day at minimum wage.

A principle that I've learnt in life is that the power to define someone is the power to control them. What I mean by this is that if you let someone else decide who you are, there is a danger of letting them set your value and control you.

Portia was caught up in an emotionally abusive relationship. Her partner was an expert at keeping her down with his words. He would constantly berate her and make fun of her council estate upbringing, telling Portia that she could never expect to attain anything of note. After all, her mother had been a victim of drugs and alcohol abuse and now all her siblings suffered the same.

What Portia did not understand was that her partner was afraid. He saw the potential in her whenever she got a promotion or raise at her job as a school dinner lady, and this unsettled him. He did not see himself going anywhere in life and if she kept up the progress she was making, perhaps one day she would wake up to the fact she was too good for him. And this terrified him.

So, he projected this fear onto Portia by telling her the worthless state he wanted her to continue in and she let him do this. She ended up doubting herself and did not go far in life, fulfilling the prophecy of her partner's words.

You must never allow anyone to define you with the words they speak, you're the one in charge of your life. Many abusers, like Portia's partner in the story above, do not even understand what they are doing. Parents, siblings and friends can tell us what they want us to be, but if this contrasts with what you are trying to become, you can refuse to let it into your mind. If you decide who you are yourself, therefore, it becomes easier for you to live up to who you have defined yourself to be.

You may be a preschool worker, but if you define yourself strictly as a preschool worker, you are containing what you can do with your life. If instead, you designate yourself as a woman of high emotion and emotional intelligence who is good with children and who happens to work in a preschool, for example, then you have a chance to see yourself going further in life. When another job role comes your way or a business opportunity that calls for those other attributes, you will not feel scared to reach out and try. If an opportunity comes out to better yourself in the area of emotional intelligence, for example, it is easier for you to follow through on that. You are able to take these attributes you defined yourself with and change yourself because you never clipped your own wings by defining yourself as a mere preschool worker.

STANDING UP FOR YOURSELF

All around you are people who want to sway you. They want to control your career for their own ends. Maybe it's a father or mother-in-law who wants to define the way they are seen in the community through your career. Perhaps it is a spouse who needs a certain social standing and he believes you need to be in a particular career to be considered a power couple. Whatever the motivation may be, family and peer pressure is a big thing in what you do for a living. There exists a certain pressure that the people who are around you try to apply. They want to define you and actually, when you think about it, it is only natural. All of us want to define what we don't understand.

Look at the way that children give others nicknames as proof. You see, the psychology behind it is, "If I can give you a nickname, and to me you become just what that nickname implies, then I have a reference point for you." The unfortunate side effect of the nicknames is that they become a self-fulfilling prophecy of sorts. A child then, who was defined as a nerd, for instance, whilst growing up confines herself only to the things that nerds are accepted as being able to do. If she fancied herself a bit of a sportswoman, she remembers that everyone called her a nerd, so she may not want to try sports.

This same type of thinking is what hampers us when we are grown up. If the people you grew up with in your estate never went to university, you must resist the easier path of skipping university as well. They may call you names, but if you realise that university is a great place to develop your career training, then go for it. Stand up for yourself in the face of the negativity and follow your dream of higher learning, instead of listening to the smarmy remarks of the people around you.

Do you know one reason why gangs thrive in the inner cities? Gangs are good at targeting and putting a definition on young people, telling them they are only good for a life of crime and violence. They don't really care for our young kids. Instead, they tell them there is no point in going to school and getting an education. If you are told this and have it demonstrated to you on a daily basis in the dreary reality of gang violence, even your resistance would be tested to breaking point. We need to have the message told that our young men and women can stand tall and define themselves. This can only happen when someone knows their worth.

Getting back to you, you need to be able to say to your dad, mum, husband, wife, boyfriend or girlfriend who you believe you are. Refuse to let their expectations define you. Some women have grown up with a perception of the kind of man they want to live with. This could be in their mind and subconsciously they are trying to mould you into this shape. Maybe it is a man of high social standing they want to be married to, or a guy with a middle-class occupation. You have to be careful about this if you do not see yourself as this kind of man. You must speak up and communicate with her, otherwise it will make for disappointment later in the relationship. Find loving ways to have conversations with those people that you care about if they are projecting crippling beliefs onto you.

You need to be able to say to your father, mother, husband, wife, boyfriend or girlfriend who you believe you are. Do not let them define you by their expectations. There are many partners who have grown up with the perception of the kind of man they want to be their partner in their head and perhaps they want mould you to become that. To them, they want to be married to a man of a high social standing, a good job. If this is not who you are, though, and that is not how you want to be defined, then you should stand up for yourself. Find ways to have conversations with your loved ones to tell them how this is crippling you.

Simon experienced this first hand with his Nigerian parents. They always told him about how they left their country of birth to come to the United Kingdom so that Simon and his sisters could have a better life. What they defined as the better life was for Simon to get a university degree of some sort. You see, in their culture, to be called a graduate was such a prestigious thing and they saw their children attaining degrees as badges of honour among their friends and family.

The trouble with this, in Simon's eyes, was how much a degree would cost compared to its value in his chosen profession. He had decided to become a chef and understudying in various Michelin star kitchens was a much better learning path for him than the Food Science degree his parents wanted him to study. He had to have the hard conversation with them without sounding disrespectful and assert his plans over his life.

HOW TO INCREASE YOUR NET WORTH

There is a difference between your intrinsic worth and your net worth. For the first part of this chapter I wanted to expand on intrinsic value. This is because who you are as a human being sits as the foundation of everything else. Any other principles of your monetary value to your workplace are made null and void if you don't believe that you matter. Net worth, then, is your value on the economic scale pertaining to money and financial assets. In short, we are talking now about money and wealth. This is probably what you wanted to know about, but believe me, that first point was important.

What is the difference between you and the successful people we see and read about? It is something I will call CONVERSION. Take this word to heart because it can be pivotal to your life if you grasp what it means. Successful people only converted the time that they had better than you did with yours. This is why they are more successful than you.

What do these names have in common? Richard Branson. Theresa May. Jessica Ennis. The cast of Geordie Shore. Jason Statham. Usain Bolt. The only difference between you and them is what they did with the resources and talents they had in their life compared to what you did with yours. This is conversion.

Let's bring this closer to home. There is no difference between you and your boss. The woman who is the CEO of your company may earn £500,000 a year and you earn £15,000, but as a person, there is nothing special about her compared to you. She is a human being and so are you. She feels sadness and you feel sadness too. She feels happiness and you feel happiness too. She feels pain and you feel pain too. She will die one day and unfortunately, so will you too. She is like you.

What then, makes her the CEO and you a low wage employee in the company? What you did with the resources that were given to you in your life so far. What did you do with your time, your money, your talents, your passions and your relationships? Your CEO used hers to further her career and make herself the best person she could be in order to get that position. If you understood how this principle works, you could increase your net worth many times over. You could even become like the people you admire the most! There are countless examples of self-made people who followed this path to success. They have mentors.

Warren Buffett, famed investor and at the time of printing, the 3rd richest person in the world, had a mentor. He discovered Benjamin Graham was teaching at Columbia Business School and took the chance to go to that institution. Consider that Buffett had already invested and saved a lot of money by the time he finished his first degree.

He did not need to look for a mentor to the untrained eye, after meeting Graham, he realised who he wanted to be as a businessman. Warren Buffett's trademark as a value investor which has made him insanely wealthy, can be attributed to him seeking out a mentor as a young man.

What I mean by conversion is taking a resource that you have like time or emotional intelligence, and then turning it, through work, into a resource that you want to have, like money. In this same way, you can convert your passion into a business. You can convert your talent into a promotion at work. This is what conversion is.

THERE IS MONEY ALREADY IN YOU

There is wealth inside you that you simply haven't converted into money yet. Due to what we have been taught in school, many of us believe that the only ways we can get money is through a job or receiving benefits. This is, however, far from the truth. You see, it is in the interest of those who run and get the most out of the ruling system to convince you to be confined to your job. After all, they need nurses to treat them when they are sick, they need teachers to teach their children and they need operators to man their machines that are producing their widgets.

Now don't get me wrong - I am not an anarchist. I've played out that scenario and have reached the practical conclusion that I'd rather have a civilised world system that protects me from Mad Max style raiders! All I do want you to see is that there are other ways to create wealth and you can tap into them as far as you would like to. You could apply these wealth increasing principles to your job, to an entrepreneurial endeavour or even to a mixture of the two, where you have a side hustle.

A lot of us believe the only way we can make money is through a job or receiving money from someone, like benefits and welfare. There is a lot of wealth in you that you are not using.

Your personality is a source of wealth in that you can capitalise on it to create services for other people that want it. If you are a cheerful and funny individual, then entertaining people can be a possible path to take. Standup comedians have taken advantage of this attribute of their personality.

Charisma is another example of a marketable attribute that

could be inside you. Some of the most prolific political leaders like Barack Obama and Tony Blair wrapped this value around their political careers to get to the highest offices in their respective lands.

We could go on to write another book simply listing the other inner values that can be converted into sources of wealth for you. Nerdiness, compassion, spirituality, wisdom, extroversion, intuition, fortitude and even diligence can all be used as a raw material to feed yourself and your family.

When you are holding your talent in your right hand, the resource of time in your left hand, and you are ready to pull up your sleeves to get to work, then making money becomes a possibility. Making a million pounds, for example, becomes an achievable feat then.

WHAT ABOUT UNHEALTHY COMPANIES?

You may ask, all this is good if you are working under good people. What about if you are in a company that has an unhealthy culture?

Company culture is an important aspect. In fact, as a rule, I don't do companies with a toxic culture anymore. My life is too short to spend with dysfunctional or crappy leaders taking me nowhere. However, I understand not everyone shares my resolve and our circumstances are not the same. Most of us can't simply afford to down tools and quit. Let me give you some advice on how to navigate the cultures and traditions of your workplace.

First, we have to define company culture. According to leadership author Andy Stanley, organisational culture is the unwritten principles or behaviours that underlie what people do in your company. Whether there is backbiting or blaming, rival departments or managers who do not play well with their subordinates, it is all culture. In the same way, openness, building colleagues up and customer focus can be cultures too.

You contribute to the culture of your company and department. Perhaps not as much as your boss, but you must take a little bit of responsibility to learn how to contribute to your workplace being a healthy environment. Whether you're naturally an introvert or an extrovert, you can purposefully work to help keep a healthy culture at work. You don't have to sacrifice what makes you unique to do it either. You can still be feisty or quiet. That does not mean that you should exasperate or tolerate unhealthy culture at work. A healthy culture, to me, is one that doesn't enjoy unnecessary conflict.

Everyone reacts to how healthy work is. When you join you can pick up on how unhealthy or healthy the culture is. Depending on how emotionally healthy you are as an individual, you will react differently to being in an unhealthy workplace. If you are healthy, you won't want to be in an unhealthy environment. You won't want to be in a job where the workers are treated as unimportant or a place where malicious gossip is the order of the day. Conversely, if you are an unhealthy individual, you will hate a healthy office or factory. If you come into a place that discourages silos and mini-tribes, and you love having a group of friends where you can talk about others, then you're going to hate working there.

Check yourself, maybe you have been changing jobs a lot. Could it be because you cannot stand healthy people around you? Are you the one who loves conflict and can't get along with people? And then you blame everyone else.

To summarise, this chapter explored what you are worth, both as a human being and in terms of monetary value. In the next chapter, we will look at practical ways in which you can increase your worth in your place of work.

THE GOLDEN NUGGETS

1. The only person who should have the power to define your life is you. Take this power back.
2. The worth of a human being is not determined by what they do for a living.

3. Net worth (which is monetary) can be increased based on what value you build in yourself.

4. You can tap into sources of wealth such as time, space and your potential if you work at it.

CHAPTER 3 – HOW TO BECOME A MASTER

Last chapter, your worth was discussed and reinforced in order to ensure that you grow a backbone. For this chapter, we are going to be exploring how, by being diligent, you, the reader, can become world class at what you do for a living. This is crucial if you are going to increase your net worth. Whether you are looking to get a promotion, to get a pay rise or to go for another job that is better for you.

BECOME AN INDISPENSABLE EMPLOYEE

Seth Godin, in his book, Linchpin: Are You Indispensable, talks about the traits that make a great employee that a company will not want to replace or get rid of:

Openness

Conscientiousness

Agreeableness

Extroversion

Emotional stability

Why should I become an indispensable employee, you may ask? This is due to the fact that, in this day and age, this is only reason that you are being paid at all! Showing up on time and simply putting in the hours in no longer enough for you to have any kind of meaningful career. In fact, if this is how you work, doing the bare minimum, if anyone better comes along or you make a mistake, you will be let go very quickly. If you work, however, in a way where you bring your best talents to work every day and you actually turn up with your personality, then you will be rewarded.

You will be promoted before other people who were in the job longer than you. You will get opportunities, together with the appropriate responsibilities and rewards, different from your peers. Your boss will invite you into his confidence. He will groom you to take over from him when he eventually gets promoted.

If you work at becoming an indispensable employee also, you will increase your value overall, so that if for any reason your job were to end, then you can take the transferable skills you have built and use them to pivot into another position or career altogether. So, you can succeed in any city, you can move to any country and still be in control of your career. Every day, new people are entering the job market, especially at entry level. The jobs that you were told in school could be yours with minimum effort, are now being fought for by migrants with a higher work ethic, students with degrees that you don't have, and older people who have more experience than you. All these people are competing with you now and if you were prudent, you would look for a way to differentiate yourself from them - become indispensable.

Leah grew up as the quintessential teacher's pet, with an uncanny ability to reproduce whatever her teachers taught her. Her friends made fun of her because she was always at the front of the class, listening attentively to whatever was coming out of the teacher's mouth.

Now, though, Leah is having the last laugh as she monetises her seemingly silly superpower. Her ability to follow instructions to the letter and attention to detail is valued by the super successful people she has worked for. She is not shallow when she has to deliver a project, she is thorough to the letter whenever she is in charge of anything. At age 35, Leah is the right-hand woman to a billionaire property investor, in charge of everything legal like deals, property acquisitions and city permits.

You too, have skills that you are ignoring, which could differentiate you from your colleagues, but you are unaware that it is valuable. If you uncover it, then take time to hone them, you can become an indispensable employee in your job.

HOW TO GET A PAY RISE

Do you want to know how to get a pay rise in the next 6 months? Talk to your boss and do the following:

1. Ask your boss what it is about you that annoys them.

2. Ask what problems they have in the department, store or factory that no one is solving for them.

3. Ask your boss to become your mentor.

At this point I can feel your cringe factor being ratcheted to max levels. Allow me to address a few points of concern. These questions must be asked with the maximum amount of humility and honesty on your part. You have to do it with the acceptance that it may not be received well. After all, your boss may not know how to take this gift you are offering. Remember, if you have never exhibited these kind of behaviours before, she may think you are up to something. Word it in the most appropriate way for the relationship you have with your boss.

I applied this in my own job and in 6 months I had the best review where I had a promotion and pay rise.

I would like to dive deeper into the 3 questions above and show you what principles are operating to get you a pay rise.

The first question is about showing you are able and even willing to receive and act on constructive feedback. Too many of us have giant egos, so we do not like feedback that our managers give us. If your boss is good at their job, they will give professional feedback that is relevant to your job and not personal. As a side note, if you cannot take any kind of criticism, do not do this step! It can backfire spectacularly if you end up in a shouting match with your boss because they hit a nerve while answering you.

Remember that your boss most probably knows what it takes to get where you want to go with your career. Perhaps it's a sideways move within the company or a straight up promotion.

I remember the day that my McDonald's store manager Mark called me, only 21 at the time, into his office and said, "Rick, we have noticed how hard you work and we want you to become a Trainer, then floor manager, with a view to you becoming a shift manager." I was totally blindsided by this and was a happy young man. He also told me, however, that I was not confident and we needed to work on that. I knew the ins and outs of flipping burgers, but I had no confidence to give instructions and directions to others. So, he wanted me to work on raising my voice and speaking up. I had major inferiority issues back then and Mark helped me to work on this.

The feeling of accomplishment that comes from even a small promotion is something I think more of us could do with. Recognition is important for complete mental health and would help many reading this book with self-esteem. More young men and women in our communities would become upstanding members of society if they applied these simple concepts and got a leg up on their career ladder.

Coming back to the 3 questions I gave above, it is necessary that you mature your emotions so that you can take feedback and improve at your job. Imagine being married to someone, but you are too immature to listen to what your wife wants you to do to help the relationship. You are doomed from the start.

The second question is powerful because it positions you as a problem solver, and more importantly, a problem solver for your boss. In life, you are paid according to the problems that you solve. If you have a job at Tesco, you get paid because you solve Tesco's problem of needing assistants to serve their customers. Tesco themselves get paid for solving the problem of people needing to buy necessities and luxury goods at affordable prices in one convenient location.

The question works to get you a pay rise on two levels. First, if your boss is in charge of pay increases, then you will want to take ownership of one or a few of his problems that you are confident you can solve. If you manage to help him and end up saving your boss time and resources then a good employer will reward you directly as soon as he can.

On the other hand, if he is not in charge (as is the case in most big companies) you still want to solve your boss's problems. You must take a more long-term view to this. If you learn the art of problem solving, you will be setting yourself up for success later on. Problem solvers are highly sought after and will be head hunted by better employers. It is easier for you to get a better job if your boss keeps taking advantage of you or blocks your intended career path. Also, problem solving makes you have something to look forward to when you get to work. The job ends up a little less boring and mundane.

The third question addresses the principle of mentoring. Mentoring is a way of getting to know what someone else knows in a shorter period, rather than if you had to go through the experiences yourself. Very few people these days take advantage of this. When you are being mentored, you are working with someone who has properly done what you want to do.

If you do it with your boss, you will be able to get into his confidence and begin to find out what he does every day. What does he do that you don't? How does he think and reason? What are his most successful methods? How does he know what he knows? Someone once said, "When you learn your boss' job, you are ready to do it yourself!" When you are closer to your boss and you become more pivotal to his own success, it puts you first in line when he is thinking about pay rises and promotions.

GOING UP THE RANKS

Earlier in this chapter, I spoke about how becoming indispensable in your job can get you a pay rise, but now let us turn our attention to promotions. Talking about becoming a master would not be complete if we did not specifically address how to get a promotion. Robert Kiyosaki, author of Rich Dad, Poor Dad, talks badly about promotions. Even though I respect his work on entrepreneurship, I am not so blasé about dismissing the power of promotion. When you get promoted, it boosts your self-confidence, it validates your hard work and it opens opportunities to make more money. There may be times when you don't want to be promoted in order to protect your time and focus, but for most people reading this book, you may want to be promoted in your job.

If you truly understand the concepts I am laying out in this book, you can go from zero to CEO of a company. It will take diligence and hard work, and every level of your journey will have its own requirements for how to move up. If you like the company you work for and believe in what they are about, then you will need to know what is required to go up in the company. Now, I'm not talking about company politics, because this is not a stable enough foundation to build your career. If you build a career on talking badly about your colleagues to the boss, then how will you run things when you are the boss and there is no one to bad mouth?

One of the things I used to do when I worked at SSE was to go to the jobs I wanted on the internal adverts and I would see what it was from the job description that I could do, couldn't do, liked doing, wouldn't like to EVER do, and what it is I could learn. When I wanted to get into IT, I visited the job pages almost daily and read the entry and low-level positions. I would note all the courses and qualifications that they wanted, the skills that they wanted and I went out and tried to get those skills.

LEARN TO DO YOUR BOSS'S JOB BETTER THAN HER

If you are going for a straightforward promotion, that is going into a position that is similar to your direct supervisor's role, then you must learn to do your boss's job better than her. If working as a customer service representative in a call centre team that is managed by a manager and a deputy manager, for instance, then you need to become aware of what these 2 positions are about and even start doing them yourself.

This is about raising your skill levels. If your manager deals with difficult customers and situations, you must start dealing with them as well.

Steve put this into practice when he started work as a

customer service advisor in an electric company contact centre. At 42, after having done many jobs he knew as he began training that he wanted to be promoted to a manager in as small a period as possible. Therefore, he went to work learning all the skills he would need as proving his competence.

Within the first three weeks of training, Steve had already surpassed his fellow trainees in understanding the core skills of a customer service advisor. The main job of his manager, he noticed, was taking over the calls that involved the most difficult customers – the dreaded "manager's call". Everyone had to pass calls to a manager once in a while and even the best advisors would get stumped by one person at least once a week. Steve, however, drew on his skills from his vast life experience to do something no one in his team had. He did not have a single manager's call in his first 6 months in the job.

Steve took it upon himself to learn the negotiation tactics and reasoning that managers needed, because he wanted to do that. After 6 months, when an opportunity arose in a different team for a deputy manager role, he was ready to apply for it, and one year after joining the company he got his first Trainee Team Manager job. In comparison, his team were still settling into life as customer service advisors and still needed to have their hands held by their manager.

If you would like to rise in the ranks fast then take a page out of

Steve's book and aggressively learn how to do the job that you want before you officially get the title. Now, get this straight, if you're crappy at your own job then you should not really be thinking about doing your boss's job. I'm a firm believer in handling your own level well before reaching for the next level. It spares you from issues further down the line. If you struggle with basic maths but decide to take a class in advanced calculus then your teacher will struggle to help you when you don't even know how the basic stuff works.

When Anne joined the WH Smith franchise at one of the M1 services, she had a personal goal. She didn't share it with anyone as it simply meant a lot to her, but her goal was that during her 3-month probation she would ensure she was fully trained in all the necessary jobs, then she would go on to become the best employee in the shop. She wanted to be better in her service to the store manager than even any of his duty managers. So, she made a little checklist of all the different jobs she had to master to ensure that she became excellent at all of them. This ranged from cleaning toilets, to stacking shelves, to mopping the shop floor. After doing this, she could concentrate at becoming the go-to night shift worker for the store. Anne knew that at this point, becoming a duty manager would be a simple transition if she fancied it.

Become number 1 at your job, then aim for the level above you. Doing your boss's job better than her is about upgrading your skills to surpass your base level. A nursing assistant may focus on assisting patients and not worry about man management. A nursing manager, however, has to focus both on treating patients and managing the team.

A good move then, is to begin to learn to manage people: informally solving problems, speaking to and helping team members and taking small things off the manager's plate. They will appreciate you for doing that. Separate yourself from everyone else in the pack and you will begin to be recognised informally as a right-hand person to your boss. It also means you can step up to the plate when your manager is not present. Too many of us are waiting to be given a promotion before we do the work but it doesn't really work that way.

Senior managers will notice what you are doing and begin to silently assess your ability to deputise your boss. When they inevitably look at promoting your boss you will be the logical replacement.

STRATEGIC SUPPORT FOR YOUR BOSS

Another way to get promoted is to help your boss get promoted. If you put on your long-term goggles and look past immediate gratification for yourself, you may see what is at work behind this principle. Study your boss and see where they want to go with their career. Now look for the job description of that role and assist your boss to get there. Make your boss look good in front of his boss. It will help you. Never embarrass the boss, even if you know more than him. This kind of action will only hurt you down the road.

No one trusts someone who is seen as being simply out for themselves. If, on the other hand, you always are making your boss look good in front of others, he will be inclined to do the same for you. You may also get taken under his wing and become privy to the inner workings of your company and your field.

If you analyse your boss's strengths and weaknesses, you will get an opportunity to work with him, according to these strengths and weakness. If you consider it carefully, there is a way that you can work with your boss's strengths, weaknesses and personality in order to create better results for him and for you. Get out of your own mind for a little while and try to understand your boss a little bit.

What is she good at? How can you multiply that? What is she weak at? How can you compensate for that? What does she enjoy? How can you incorporate this into how you do your job? In other words, accentuate your boss's strengths and make her into a star but also help her weaknesses. Selflessness will help your career in the long run. If your strengths are complimentary to her weak points, then prop up that side of her so that she can concentrate on what she does best.

If you have a shred of awareness of your work environment, you will know that your manager or supervisor has a particular personality and trait. You naturally learn how to stay out of their way when they are not happy and how to work well with them when they are happy. It is to your benefit to avoid unnecessary conflict with your boss. In real terms, they affect you more than most of the other people in your life. Like it or not, the boss affects your money through your salary and they also affect the atmosphere at the place where you spend a third of your day! You cannot get around the fact that clashing with the boss all the time will make both of your lives miserable.

In my first IT job, I had a couple of managers who were very different. I'll call them Hans and Mike. Hans was free-wheeling and jocular in nature, but when we were busy, he was no nonsense. For 98% of the time when he was in a good mood, I would riff with him quite a bit but when the job got busy I knew to get my head down, not mess around, and I would go into do mode. I never took his easy-going nature for granted or made him look bad for trusting us to do our jobs with little direct supervision.

Mike, on the other hand, was a fatherly figure who saw it as his personal mission to get me to the level of competence I needed to be technically. He got into my personal space and looked over my shoulder a lot. To him, managing meant mollycoddling his young wards. He needed me to talk to him constantly so he could gauge what I needed to do my job better. When I realised this, I let him do it. I was a trainee and I was humble enough to work with him in the manner that was best for him. It was no skin off my back at the end of the day and I actually grew to enjoy having him as a safety net in case I did something wrong.

How did I know this about my two managers? I observed them and thought about it when I was at home. I asked my colleagues who had worked with them for years. And I listened when the men were talking and drew conclusions from what they talked about.

So, to finish off the chapter we saw that, if you would like to, you can become an indispensable employee and chart your career to heights that you want. Mastery, however, will take hard and smart work. In the next section, we will take the concept of work to another level by seeing what to do if you are not working in the right job.

THE GOLDEN NUGGETS

1. In order to excel in your job, you must become an indispensable employee.
2. A pay rise is a simple thing to make happen if you consider what problems you can solve for your boss or employer.
3. To get a promotion at work, you must learn how to do the job you want before you get there and then start demonstrating that to your supervisor.

4. If you become an asset to your boss, strategically supporting him/her in their role, you will put yourself in a better position to succeed.

PART 2 – CALLING AND PURPOSE

"You can't just sit there and wait for people to give you that golden dream, you got to get out there and make it happen for yourself."

Diana Ross

CHAPTER 4 – DO YOU HAVE PURPOSE?

In the last section, we spoke about what to do to make the most of working a low wage or minimum wage job. This section will be about looking at work differently and avoiding slaving away in a job forever. Even though this book is called Minimum Wage Revolution, I don't think anyone should aspire to be doing a minimum wage job forever. What I am saying instead, is yes, you have a minimum wage job but what is the next step for you? You could go the route described in the last section of working your current job until it yields a better role for you, or you can find something else that makes you feel alive.

Research has found that if people are doing a job that is not in their passion, they will not be likely to enjoy it for long. They will also, consequently, be unlikely to do well at it, which further contributes to them not enjoying it. This, then, is where PURPOSE comes in.

The question of purpose has troubled humankind for thousands of years. Do you ever wonder what you are on planet earth for? I'm not really a fan of the theory that it's all for nothing that we live in the world. The fact that I am a thinking and reasoning being makes me want to reach for bigger and better purpose for me and my children.

The Oxford dictionary defines purpose as:

1. The reason for which something is done or created or for which something exists.

2. A person's sense of resolve or determination.

I like to look at purpose as the reason for which you exist, which you have resolved to carry out with your life. Your purpose is what you are on this planet for. I think it is no coincidence that those people who achieve massive success in their lives usually have a strong sense of purpose. I'm talking world and nation changers. Churchill, to an extent, believed he was born at the time he was so that he could fight Nazi Germany. Florence Nightingale saw herself as having been put in her professional to tend to the wounded.

There is a nagging question in most of us asking if this is all that our existence is meant for. Is the sum total of your days on earth just to wake up, take a dump, have breakfast, kiss your wife and kids, go to work, have sex, eat, watch TV, laugh at some jokes and try to have more sex? Is that all there is to life?

EXAMINING YOUR LIFE HISTORY

Another way of finding out what your life purpose is, is to examine your life history. Here you will find clues about yourself hidden away.

Many of us don't like looking at our life history because there could be pain, embarrassing memories or even shame hidden there. So, we suppress the whole memory. However, I honestly believe that there are things that happened to you in the past, which if pulled apart and unraveled, could have clues into who you are.

Is there anything hidden in your past that could be a clue?

There was a time that I found myself in dire straits. My marriage had imploded, my business was in tatters, I had no job and I was completely broke. Because of this, I took six months to sort my life out. I refused to go back into a high activity career because I found myself in a brand new city and I wanted to see what else I could do with my life. So, with a new low wage job doing newspaper deliveries, I started mulling over my past. Looking at my childhood, and in particular the school years, I remembered the things I had been teased about. I have always had a big head and used to be quite self-conscious about its size and spherical shape. It is very round – when I shave my head it looks like a brown football. I got called names like Sperm (apparently my massive head compared to my skinny body resembled one).

All this was naturally quite hurtful, however, as I grew up and became more confident in my teens I began to focus more on this head that everyone talked about. It struck me that I had a slightly higher IQ than my peers. Obviously, this had nothing to do the exact volume of my skull but the stigma from the name-calling got me to focus on what was inside my head - my brain. So I focused on intellectual pursuits, reading and I enjoyed daydreaming and imagination. I didn't focus too much on physical activity, but began to expand my imagination through watching television and adventure cartoons. I spent days looking at maps of the world and imagining what those areas were like. I broadened my horizons and became adept at language and mental pursuits.

How, may you be asking, did this help me when I was reflecting? I returned to my roots of writing and thinking. I began to use my writing skills to articulate what I had learnt and this book was the result. I also started writing for my favourite personal development mentors and a few of them asked me to do it for them in a professional capacity. So, a second income stream materialised doing something I enjoyed much more than staring at spreadsheets at my old job.

PURPOSE MAKES FOR AN EXCITING LIFE

Knowing what you are designed for makes for a more interesting life. Things are more fun when you see life this way. Let me show you why. First of all, you are going to be naturally good at the thing that you were designed to do. It is a pleasant feeling to be naturally good at something. You don't have to work as hard at it as everyone else and when you do want to become masterful at it (which will require hard work), it doesn't feel like hard work to you. Second, you laugh and smile much more as you do the thing you are naturally inclined to. You are less stressed when doing something you are excited about.

Gerard used to be miserable before he joined the world of local politics. After finishing college, he did not feel that the subjects he studied were interesting to him. His dad had helped him choose and unfortunately, they had chosen wrong. English, economics and technology were not the party he had hoped they would be. One day, however, Gerard was invited to a Green Party meeting where he saw another world completely.

Here he found people who were interested in the environment and taking care of the poor. He began to debate and pit his own ideas against those that were opposed and this was exhilarating. Gerard's weekends away campaigning and exchanging world views with young people like him was the ultimate preparation to go into political studies. This kind of

education made much more sense to him and he looked
forward to going to university after saving for his life there.

In the above parable, Gerard found his purpose in political studies, which fired him up to want to engage in education again. If more of the young people of our nations were steered to find purpose instead of working in a job for the sake of it, there would be far happier and better performing pupils in schools, colleges and universities.

WHAT DO YOU LIKE TO DO?

When was the last time that you asked yourself what you like or enjoy doing? With the way work and life is always busy, we never stop to ask ourselves what we like. It is necessary for you to make a habit to sit down and assess what brings you enjoyment and fun when you do it. It could turn out to be the simple things like your hobbies, but at least ask yourself the question.

This process is part of exploring your purpose. Don't get me wrong, purpose is not found from some exterior mystic force but from within yourself. What brings you joy and makes you the happiest? Be honest with yourself. Answers that are based on society's or your friends' expectations will not cut it. Don't fall into the trap of what you believe a man should say, or a woman should say. Just because you think a proper woman should enjoy taking care of her children doesn't mean you should answer in this way. You are much more than your parental responsibilities. If playing tennis, for example, gets your juices flowing, then own it!

At what point is your adrenaline pumping and endorphins getting released? Pinpoint that. Of course, if what you enjoy hurts your body, health or risks your life needlessly, then maybe it is not the right thing to be focusing on. I know a girl who really liked bossing people around. She went out and looked for the types of jobs that involved doing this every day. She found out that as a manager, you could tell people what to do and get paid well for it. The army turned out to be the perfect place for her and that's where she went. Now she's happily giving orders.

WHAT ARE YOU GOOD AT?

One of the simplest and most straightforward ways to find your purpose in life is to figure out what you are naturally good at. What do you think you do best? What do the closest people to you think you are best at? What do people compliment you on often? What is the thing that doesn't take that much out of you when you do it? The kind of thing that is inside you and naturally flows out.

Emeli Sande, famed Scottish songwriter and singer, was a talented musician as a child. From her days writing a song for a primary school talent show at the age of 11, Emeli knew she had a talent for music. This also coincided with her desire to be a professional musician and she persisted with her dream, even while studying to be a medical doctor.

It may seem obvious now but Emeli Sande had to battle her parents who had a very old-fashioned view that it was too difficult to make a living in music. She had to lean on the fact that she was good at her craft, relying both on the natural musical talent she possessed and a hard work ethic, unlike any of her contemporaries. Due to this, her success was only a matter of time, culminating in her being awarded an MBE for her services to music.

Not only can this happen to Emeli Sande, but to anyone reading this book who is able to work out what they are good at and then work at it like their life depended on it.

When you had a review at work, what did your boss tell you that you were good at? You can find a way of expanding on this attribute of yours and turning it into a part of your career. I will expand on this further in a later chapter on having a side hustle.

Is there anything you can do with the least amount of preparation? Perhaps because you live and breathe that topic all the time anyway? If I am asked to answer a question or write a short piece on a topic like entrepreneurial solutions to my city's issues, I don't need to read a book but can do it. If I am asked to give a keynote speech on jobs and work, I can just get going with minimum prep. In the same way that Peter Thiel would not hesitate if asked to talk on contrarian behaviour in the economy, so do you have an area that you're naturally good at. What you naturally thrive at is a clue into what you need to be doing with your life. You may not yet be good enough to make any money from it, but it is a glimpse into your purpose.

EVERYONE IS A GENIUS, SOMETIMES

I have a very helpful mental exercise I go through from time to time. Have you ever done something right? Even once? We all have. Maybe you have to stretch your memory all the way to your childhood and school to find the inspiration. Go back to the past to remember how you did that thing. Was it a test you once passed? Did you come first at any competition? Did you set yourself a goal to talk to a girl that you were scared of and then do it? Did you master a song on an instrument?

When I was 15 years old, I emerged in my school year as the best at maths. It was so drastic that I got the nickname "Doc" from my classmates. This all happened because a year before that, my aunt sat me down when I showed her my mediocre end of year exam paper. Through simple explanations, she showed me that I had been randomly approaching the questions, but if I went through the problems methodically, I would get the right answers. I realised that I had known the correct answers all along, but because I had not structured my thinking, I struggled. Over the next two years, I applied the correct structure and practiced my maths daily, becoming the best student in my class.

The true magic for me started happening as I grew older. I began to learn new skills in this same way by applying the same method of looking for basic structure or principle, then practicing like hell. I have done this with writing. I have done it with creating social media content. Every day and with each project, I get better. I am doing it with money management where I am daily learning new principles for saving and investing money, then applying them. We all have a genius inside us.

To conclude this chapter, we saw that there are reflective questions you can ask in order to get clues into what your purpose in life is, whether that is looking back into your past, asking those around you for feedback or checking your gut inclinations. In the next chapter, I will go further to see how you can channel these findings into an endeavour to do apart from your job.

THE GOLDEN NUGGETS

1. Clues to your purpose in life are hidden in your history, background and experiences, even the bad stuff that happened to you.

2. Figure out what you enjoy doing and what you are good at as these things will be easier for you to work at. You will enjoy going to work when you identify these things.

3. Every person has something that they are a genius at, some of the time. Life's challenge is doing the mental work to find it.

RICK MATSOKOTERE

CHAPTER 5 - THE SIDE HUSTLE

When you have uncovered your purpose, as we figured out how to do in the previous chapter, a side-hustle apart from your job can be an option for following that passion.

At times, you will find it difficult to just stay in a job. Sometimes you want to be more. If I want to become a millionaire, I cannot just stay in a job in McDonalds; I have to do some other things. At McDonalds, in 10 years, I can be a director making £100,000 but it will be tough to make millions in that job. So, what are the ways of going out and making things happen?

This chapter is about doing a side hustle alongside your low wage job. I describe a side hustle as another stream of income that you place alongside your main breadwinning work. It is a hustle because it is hard and requires extra effort and smart thinking to make it work.

The truth is that the opportunities to do other things on the side are endless. There is such an up side to what you can do with your life, that I had to give the idea its own chapter in the book. A side hustle is a good way to take advantage of your purpose while you are stuck in your job - for now.

YOU HAVE TO BE PRACTICAL

Not everyone is in the situation where they are in a minimum wage job they enjoy and so are willing to work patiently until they rise through the ranks. What if the job really doesn't do it for you?

The reality is that, for most people working a low wage job, it isn't their first choice of what they would rather be doing. It is definitely not a calling for the average person! Unfortunately, however, we can't all just quit these jobs and do our own thing.

To start with, it doesn't make financial sense for most of us. The truth on the ground is that many ordinary workers are in a very bad financial state personally with consumer debt, mortgages, negative equity and overspending being the order of the day. Even those of us who try to live within our means are, because of a low wage, struggling to make enough to survive. This alone is a good reason to think about taking matters into our own hands and getting a side hustle going.

People who are involved in the minimum wage revolution are realising they could do a couple of things alongside their job. It can supplement your income. Not everyone who became involved in a side enterprise is doing it to become a millionaire. For most, it is all about being practical. This is what this book is about. Even though I talk about solid principles I try to keep it as down to earth and practical as possible. It is very practical to do your business outside work hours - at least to begin with - rather than to quit your job cold turkey! You must be responsible towards your spouse, your kids and think about the house, fees and the bills you have to pay in everyday life.

WE CAN'T COMPLAIN IN THE 21ST CENTURY

If you are reading this book, chances are that you have a little bit of disposable income. If this describes you, then you, just like me, cannot be complaining! This century is full of opportunities. Due to globalisation and technological advances, chances to do something for yourself at a cheap cost are endless.

Consider the world of education with me. What, 15 years ago, would take someone 4 years to learn in a prestigious institution of learning like the London School of Economics, an African, an Indian or a South American can now access with a smartphone and 4G. Information or knowledge is now available to everyone through the internet. I share videos on creating personal wealth that are watched by people as far afoot as Zimbabwe. What I want you to see is that there is now an open playing field as to changing your life to what you want to achieve and people around the world who have far less resources than you are getting things done while you complain.

Social media (the slang term for the current state of the internet) has brought the infinite opportunities of the world into the palm of your hand. Most of the life changing ideas I get these days are in my bedroom, through my iPad or phone. My friend, there are people in India cutting down coconuts with a machete and then selling that coconut water in England. We have people who are making and selling t-shirts from the basement of their mother's house. Women are going to car boot sales, buying things for £1 and then selling them for £6 on eBay.

Others are achieving so much on a side hustle that you don't have the right to complain. When you complain, you have a vision of something that you want but are not willing to risk creating. Even if you are on unemployment benefits, that money can be your starting capital. You have to bite the bullet and cut out some time and money wasting crap in order to get your side hustle going.

Muhammad Yunus is a Bangladeshi banker and recipient of the Nobel Peace Prize (2006) and credited with developing the concepts of microfinance and microcredit. These are schemes which offer small loans to the rural poor – to enable them to invest and lift themselves out of poverty.

During Yunus' research into rural poverty, he found that many poor labourers, especially women, had no access to bank loans. Therefore, they resorted to unofficial loan sharks, who charged excessive rates of interest. This meant poor entrepreneurs were either unable to get a loan or were stuck in paying off very high interest charges. Yunus felt there was a gap in the market, and if poor entrepreneurs had access to finance at low interest rates, it would help investment and wealth creation. Yunus believed that if loans were affordable, people would be able to pay back the loans and it would be self-financing.

He decided, therefore, to lend some of his own money to 42 women in the village of Jobra, near Chittagong, Bangladesh. It was only a total of US$27, and he was repaid with a profit of $0.02 on each loan. This convinced him microloans were a viable business model. After this, Microfinance as a concept has spread to over a 100 mostly developing countries around the world.

If people in Bangladesh and Zambia are finding ways to make it work, then you have no right to complain, my friend.

LITERALLY A MILLION WAYS TO WIN

Gary Vaynerchuk, CEO of Vayner Media and social media guru, wrote his first book Crush It in 2009. In it, Gary Vee showed people were using a side hustle to get what they wanted. He profiled people who were, like he did, working a job from 9-6, spending a few hours with their family, then spending 7pm-2am building the dream they had on the side. After two or three years of consistent action, these people were living their passion and their purpose. This is the power of a side hustle in the minimum wage revolution.

Bringing all this back to practicality, how do you actually build a business on the side? I like to start from the law of income which states that you are paid according to the problems you solve. When it comes down to it, any side hustle you are doing has to be solving a problem for someone somewhere. Before you go anywhere else, you can look at your own community. What problems are there in your local community that people are willing to pay you to solve?

The way I break it down is like this: If you live in a small to medium sized city, there are at least 7 spheres or areas that you can be involved in. Money or Business. Entertainment. Government. Education. Religion. Media. And Family.

There is a money system or economy that runs through the heart of your city. The entertainment scene of your city. Government is the sphere of those that rule the city. The city council, law enforcement, the judiciary and legislators. Our children and even adults are equipped for the future through the education sphere. Society is based on the building blocks of families. Destroy families and there is no society to speak of. The media that reports the truth of what is happening in the city. The role religion and faith plays in the moral fabric of your city.

If you look at these areas, you should be able to find a couple that you are interested in, or better yet, passionate about that you can look to serve. If you sit down and do the work to ask some questions, you can provide solutions within those spheres. Match the skills you have recognised in yourself with one of those spheres and you will have the field you are best equipped to build your business.

BECOME A MEDIA COMPANY AND LET THE WORLD KNOW

The last step of building your side business is to tell everyone what you are doing. If you want to make any money at all, you have to have customers, clients, partners or sponsors to what you are doing, and this applies for non-profit initiatives too. In order to attract these people to your idea, you cannot get around telling them about it. Yes, your personality may determine how you go about doing this, but it still needs to be done.

It is all good and fine doing all the above work to build a platform, but if no one knows what you are doing or how you differ from everyone else on the market, then you are going nowhere fast. The internet right now gives you the opportunity to become a media company. DJ Khaled, Logan Paul, Connor Maynard and Dwayne Johnson have all decided to own the message they send out to their audience.

With me, I study, practice and talk about knowledge and wisdom. I then use media like videos and articles to showcase this wisdom. Are you funny, or poignant, or relevant, or insightful, or energetic, or passionate, or emotional? Learn how to channel all this in order to get people to see what you are doing in your side hustle.

In a nutshell, this chapter has been about how there are a countless number of ways to get going with a side-hustle. This could supplement or even eventually replace your job, allowing you to live your dream. In the next section, we will look at the greatest resource you have at your disposal to make these dreams of yours come true.

THE GOLDEN NUGGETS

1. In order to follow your purpose, you will have to be practical about your responsibilities and perhaps start a side project.
2. The 21st century has many opportunities available to us, especially since the advent of the internet.
3. Just about any hobby, interest, burden or passion you may have can be turned into a business, non-profit or organisation.

4. In order to get what you are doing off the ground, you will need to start broadcasting what you have using the new media avenues available.

RICK MATSOKOTERE

PART 3 – TIME: LIFE'S GREATEST RESOURCE

> *"The common man is not concerned about the passage of time, the man of talent is driven by it."*
>
> *Shopenhauer*

CHAPTER 6 – USING TIME TO YOUR ADVANTAGE

In the previous part of the book, we saw how it is possible to find out what your purpose in life is while you are in a minimum wage or entry level job and then pivot into following that as a career. This is if working your job is not for you. In this chapter, however, I will be showing you the resource that you have to create your desired life – time.

A valuable life lesson I have learnt, is that time is a potentially powerful resource that you have at your disposal. When in a minimum wage job, you have to count the things that are on your side and one of them is time. The way I will unpack will probably be different to anything that you have heard before.

There is some truth in the old adage - Life is unfair. I'm under no illusions that sometimes you are born into a lower class or other unfortunate circumstances. In this case, then, you may not have the silver spoon that you think others have. Being born to the "right" parents makes people around you get special favours you may not have. Some people got an education. Others got contacts and connections through their family. Other kids got an inheritance. Perhaps other people got loans from their folks to get a head start over you. You can even go as far as to say being born in certain countries is like hitting the lottery. It is undeniable a boy born in the United States, the United Kingdom or Germany has far better prospects to make something of himself than that same boy born in Somalia, Zimbabwe or Iraq.

The best counter to being in unfortunate circumstances that I have found, however, is that there is one thing that all men and women everywhere have. It is a resource called time and all of us have the same amount every day - 24 hours. The reason that this theme is coming into play in this book on work and jobs is that there is only one tool that we have at our disposal to mine the treasure hidden in time, that is WORK. This book is all about the power of work, specifically as it pertains to those who have lower wage jobs, so I would like to lay out the principles that I believe will help you to make the most of yourself using time, just as I did.

TIME IS LIFE AND LIFE IS TIME

What is the most important possession you have? Perhaps life itself is number one. Without it, nothing else matters. The fact that you breathe today is what enables you to do everything else, like have a family, think, make money or read this book. All you have is the one life and you must enjoy it and live it well. What would happen, then, if you did an experiment and broke this life down?

If you broke life down into its component parts, you would find time to be the core material. Your life is a sum of however many years you will live. Those years consist of twelve months each. Each month has a certain number of days and within each day is hidden 24 hours. Hours are made up of minutes and seconds. This is what your life and my life eventually come down to, hence time is the raw material for life.

From this logic, it follows and I would like to suggest to you to look at time and life interchangeably. Time is life. And life is time. When you think of your life, it seems like a massive thing, but when you consider the passing seconds you realise it isn't that much. Every minute that passes is never coming back to you and in fact brings you ever closer to the day of your death.

Therefore, the way you use your time is crucial. You must look at it as the very essence of life.

24 HOURS IS ALL WE HAVE

What do you and Theresa May have in common? You have 24 hours in your day and so does she. How about you and Richard Branson? 24 hours. What do you and Wayne Rooney have in common? You guessed it: 24 hours in each of your days! The only difference in why these people have more in terms of money, influence and material success than you, is what they did with their 24 hours over a consistent period of time. Wayne spent virtually all his teens and twenties chasing after a ball and practicing doing special things with it.

WASTING, SPENDING OR INVESTING TIME

I hope what I have said so far in this chapter has stressed to you how important time is. I don't want to sound like a crazy conspiracy theorist, but if you do not rush to determine and control what you do with your time, someone else will do it. They will invent distractions, entertainment and pastimes that ensure you spend your life (and money) on what they want you to. Time, as we have determined, is precious because it is the essence of life itself. Who controls what you do with your time?

Here's an example of a model day:

A day is made up of 24 hours. A typical person wakes up every morning and 8am to 6pm are the prime times of their day. Normally, you are working your job during this time. The other times are not as valuable and there are the times you spend with your family, engaging in your hobbies and sleeping.

The question you must ask is, Am I selling the prime real estate of my day for peanuts?

The hours between 8am and 6pm are the prime real estate of your day. These are the hours that you are most productive and you have highest energy levels. Your brain, during these times, is functioning at its peak. It is also the best time to get things done because other people are in work mode during this time.

In a low wage job, you are exchanging this prime real estate in packaged chunks to your employer for £7.50, £10 or even £15 per hour. Is this amount worth your prime time? In the last section of the book we discussed how you can find your purpose and place on the earth. I really think that it is better to use your prime time to advance that cause of yours.

For the sake of practicality, I realise that most of the readers of this book are reading because they are in a low wage. However, is your job the best use of that time? Could you alternatively be building something that fulfils your life purpose in the core hours of the day and then doing a job to pay the bills outside those hours?

WHAT DO YOU DO WITH YOUR SPARE TIME?

It is just a fact, however, that most of us have to work a job between 9am and 5pm. If we could afford to quit, many would, but it is just impossible with our existing commitments. The only other place you can get time is after 5 or 6pm. If you do a shift pattern or nights, you can adjust the times to suit your situation. What do you do after 6pm? Do you simply go to bed and sleep? Do you watch television or YouTube videos? Are you always out? Do you always find yourself hanging out with friends?

It is important that you pinpoint what you do with your hours after work. The rest of your day is the second-best slab of time and I recommend using this time to make your dreams come true. I am writing this particular part of this book on a Sunday morning before I go to work for a night shift later. I could be having a lie in but I want to make a product that is valuable and worth spending your hard-earned money to buy. Hence, I do the hard things necessary and make use of my time wisely.

The key I want you to understand here is that you can use the free time you have to do something that will free up your prime time later in life. The goal will be that, if you make things happen for 5 years, you will be able to quit the job you don't enjoy to do what you love for the rest of your life. It will be a powerful exercise to intentionally think about your time. Do you really think about your time?

Gary Vaynerchuk is one of the most famous people you haven't heard of on social media. He is a master of internet trends and understands how to use them to promote whatever business you may have. He runs the agency Vayner Media which helps large companies around the world use Facebook, Instagram and Snapchat, among other platforms, to build their sales through branding.

Gary was not always the brash, swashbuckling personality that his enormous fan base loves today. He started it all by using time to build his father's business while no one was watching, then he appeared on the scene like an overnight success. The more observant eye, however, will see quickly that there is nothing "overnight" about his success.

Born in Belarus to a Russian Jewish family, Gary and his parents emigrated to the United States when he was 3 years old, where they lived with several other family members in a tiny studio apartment. His father, Sasha, became a stock boy at a liquor store and worked his way up until he was the manager of the store. He and his wife saved up all the money they got and he finally bought his own liquor store in Edison, New Jersey.

At 14, Gary was bought in to work on weekends bagging ice and it wasn't long until his talent for selling was noticed. At 24, after graduating college, Gary was handed the reigns of the store. By day, Vaynerchuk worked tirelessly selling on the shop floor, figuring out emerging technologies like email marketing and Google Adwords and training his team to build one of the first online wine stores in the world. He spent four or five hours each day after the normal nine hours to build this skill set.

The result of all this extra work was that he built his father's business from a $3 million to a $60 million business in a period of 6 years. He started the first ever wine show on YouTube in the first year of the platform's existence and so began his career with social media sites. To this day, when Gary is asked how he became so good at marketing on the internet, he insists that it is the extra time he spends each day trying things out and learning the new platforms. This is what he does with his spare time and he has created companies and personal brands worth hundreds of millions of dollars.

What you are worth on a personal level is directly linked to the things that you do with your spare time. Do you waste that time or do you invest it in increasing your knowledge in your chosen field?

In summary, we saw in this chapter that time is your very life and every minute that you waste is wasted life. In the next chapter, we will see how you can patiently use time to build yourself into an expert on anything you choose.

THE GOLDEN NUGGETS

1. Time is the most precious resource that you have at your disposal, as it is the raw material that life is made from.

2. What you do with your 24 hours in each day is the difference between your failure and your success.

3. Fools waste time, mediocre people spend time and wise people invest their time. You are currently operating in one of these categories.

4. After your job and family commitments, there are hours of spare time that you have to apportion towards making yourself a better person. Avoid using these for trivial pursuits.

RICK MATSOKOTERE

CHAPTER 7 – PATIENCE AND CONSISTENCY

Last chapter, the concept of time was broken down to prove how time is not a trivial thing to treat frivolously, but instead it is the most precious resource you have. Now, we will focus more on the positive changes you can effect on your career using time patiently and consistently.

If there is anything that life will teach you, is you do not get everything that you want straight away. Patience and consistency of action is a critical requirement. The work of becoming successful demands it! Something important that time carries within it is the promise that if you are consistent with the right actions, eventually the results will come. And in a low wage job, you have that luxury to be able to work in obscurity, while everyone ignores you to their own peril.

The issue in today's society, however, is that we want immediate results. We truly underestimate what we can do with a decade and what a decade can bring out of us. Yes, you may be in a minimum wage job today, but over many years, you will be able to prove yourself to be worth something in whatever endeavour you concentrate.

YOU WILL GET YOURS

I used to have this fantasy: that I would start in a job and within a year, I'd be a manager and two years after that I would be CEO. Many of us have variations of this fantasy:

"If I come up with a money saving innovation the, company will promote me right away."

"If I laugh at the jokes my manager makes, he will make me supervisor."

"If I say my name enough times in front of my manager, he will promote me when the next slot opens up."

"If I befriend all the managers, they will make me one of them in no time."

Unfortunately, chances are these things are not going to happen. There are just so many moving parts that have to align for you to rise through the ranks, if this is your goal.

If you learn the power of patience, however, you will eventually get what's coming to you. With time, your efforts start to get recognised, your name will come up in favourable conversations enough times and the authenticity of your work will rise to the top. Did you know that in the next 10 years, around 30% of leadership positions in organisations are going to be up for grabs in various fields around the world? This will happen because people die, people retire and organisations change.

The question is, are you doing anything to position yourself where you can get into any of these positions? Instead of being impatient about how nothing is opening up for you right now, you could be doing something to develop yourself so that you are ready to step into the position when it does open up.

Malcolm Gladwell, in his book Tipping Point, found that people who put in 10,000 hours into their talent end up becoming world class at it. Consider this for a minute. If you put in 10,000 hours of whinging and complaining, you will become a world class whinger and complainer. If you put in 10,000 hours of doing the bare minimum and showing up late for work, that is what you will become world class in.

However, if you put in 10,000 hours of going above and beyond the call of duty, extraordinary customer service, applying emotional labour to your job then you will be world class at that. What would you rather be world class at?

WHERE CAN YOU GET 10,000 HOURS?

You may be asking right now. 10,000 hours? Where can I get that kind of time? Here is how it roughly breaks down if you work 40 hours a week:

10,000 hours is 250 weeks.

250 weeks is about 5 years (52 weeks a year).

So, if you really enjoy your job making beds in a hotel, after 5 years you will have become better at it than 99% of people out there. At this point, nothing is stopping you becoming a trainer in this area of hospitality or specialising to become a consultant for hotels around the country.

Now, it's totally possible that you are not in the job of your dreams and you have decided to work in the direction I spoke of in Chapter 5 of having a side hustle. 10,000 hours in this endeavour will help you make it into something you are world class at. Let's break down those hours to see what it would look like if you came home after work and spent 3 hours a day for 5 days of the week on your side business:

15 hours in a week

750 hours in a year

10,000 hours in 13 years!

If you dedicate 5 hours a day (perhaps 8pm to 1am) for 5 days a week:

25 hours in a week

1250 hours in a year

10,000 hours in 8 years!

In reality then, you can become a world class online seller, interior designer or programmer all from your low wage job if you simply have patience and put in consistent work.

If you look at life from a big picture perspective, you will realise that this principle is exactly what your 20s, 30s and 40s are for. It just depends how old you are as you read this book. Professional sportspeople who break out as stars at 18 or 20 years old have usually spent a decade giving up their years to be dedicated to their sport. Lebron James, possibly the best to play basketball since Michael Jordan, did not just appear on the scene at the NBA draft and surprise everyone. He wasn't an overnight success. At age 7, he was at the court working on his skills, running, jumping and dribbling the ball. This is what your teens are for if you are a young ambitious person reading this book.

Those people who broke out in their 30s spent the bulk of their 20s putting in their 10,000 hours. Many career people like lawyers, doctors and engineers become high-flyers in their 30s. Readers who have finished university or college and are just starting out should understand this. In your 20s you may not have much, but that is fine and in fact, to be expected. These years are for you to put in your 10,000 hours in the company or in your profession. The 10,000 hours I spent in major corporations in the UK throughout my 20s prepared me to write this book and go out and start my businesses.

The majority of millionaires and billionaires break out in their 40s. The main reason is that they dedicate their 30s to becoming rich and so building their business. See if this story doesn't make sense: a young man who spends his 20s finding himself and his purpose, gets serious after 30 and becomes a workaholic, starting and developing a company that becomes a market leader when he is in his 40s. This time spent building value in himself and in his company, is what makes him a rich man.

And don't forget those late bloomers who make it in their career after 50. Many of us spend the first half of our lives in a daze, but after something catastrophic happens to us like divorce, a middle-life crisis or the death of someone close, we wake up and decide to spend our 40s putting in the required 10,000 hours. Fame and riches come thereafter in our 50s.

Ian Marchant was the CEO of Scottish and Southern Energy during the years that I worked there and he was an inspiration to me. In 1992, he arrived at the company as an accountant from Ernst and Young. One of the members of his small team asked what his career goals were when he arrived. Ian famously quipped, "I aim to be nothing less than the CEO of this company in ten years!" In 2002, ten years after joining the company, Ian Marchant was appointed CEO of Scottish and Southern Energy and reigned over one of the corporations most profitable seasons.

The simple realisation I am trying to bring to you is that it is never too late for you to use the 10,000-hour principle. You simply need to sit down with your thoughts, decide what it is you want to focus those hours and that dedication to and just go. This ties in with the theme of Part 2 of this book. If you find your life purpose, you will find an area that you love so much that you won't even notice the 10,000 hours flying past. I am a writer but I am very particular about the topics I write on. I enjoy personal development and leadership themes and when I write about them, the time simply flies past. I would hate to write, for instance, a fiction novel right now, because that genre just doesn't inspire me as much.

WHAT'S MORE IMPORTANT? THE PROCESS VS THE REWARD

When time is passing and you are working hard, what's happening behind the scenes is that you are slowly becoming a person of value. If you set yourself a target to become a manager or even director of your company by age 35, for example, achieving this goal will be an awesome thing. However, upon closer inspection, there is a more important aspect which is what kind of person you become in the process.

There are characteristics and qualities that make a good director and you will find that unconsciously, you have built them within yourself. Maybe you started not being able to speak to people that well, but with time, you have become more empathetic, a better listener and you start to lead people instead of bossing them around.

This here is what I call the importance of the process over the rewards. Becoming a millionaire is less about the £1 million, but about the things you have to change internally while you're doing it. This is why a self-made millionaire or billionaire can make the money again after a catastrophe, but a lottery winner will probably lose the money and never get it again.

CONSISTENT ACTION BUILDS MASSIVE SUCCESS

You do not make use of time by simply sitting there, scratching your head and doing nothing. Instead, you have to put in hard and smart work in order to build up massive success. The key is that by stringing your action through consistency, you build momentum. Some people have put in action, got some measure of success or failure, and then they stopped! This has in turn killed their momentum and brought the good coming their way to a halt. You must keep going and build on your successes, bulldozing through your failures along the way. When you get one result and then another, this will lead to a snowball effect.

It is important to be a finisher. Anyone can start something, but how many people are finishers? If you have ever finished anything important in your life, no matter how small, you are better than most. I recently worked with a young man who walked out at his job in a shop. Just before that he had walked out on his probation period at McDonalds. He just could not finish anything he started with regards to working a job.

This phenomenon happens a lot in minimum wage jobs. Many people don't finish what they start. Or they start educational courses and don't finish. The same goes with projects. Is there a pattern of not finishing in your past? This will affect you from getting pay rises and promotions. In fact it will affect you in jobs to the point where you leave if you feel any discomfort.

However, this is not the way to deal with all discomfort. Some discomfort is caused by growing pains. Life is resisting you to force you to develop. If you leave, though, you will not grow.

So, have you ever finished anything? If you have to, you can pull out a mundane example from your memory.. The importance of this is that I want to prove that you are better in this respect than many people on earth who don't finish anything. Most good managers appreciate someone who starts a piece of work and finishes it properly. All successful people that I know of are looking for finishers who can carry out their instructions well.

Successful people are not looking for talkers with the gift of the gab, but looking for finishers who can complete tasks and projects. This is a basic skill requirement if you want to shine while in a minimum or low wage job. I challenge you to put some proper time into one job. Set yourself the goal of not leaving the job you are in currently until you become a manager, for instance. Or give yourself a time frame with a few goals within that. I guarantee you the results of that will be good for you. You will be able to use the achievement of that goal in interviews for other jobs that you go for later. A finished project that you have done will go into your portfolio and this will be impressive when you have to prove your professional chops.

You must graduate into maturity and time can be your ally in this. Immature people are always jumping from one job to the other, taking and causing offence wherever they go. Immature people will, unfortunately, always stay at the bottom of the food chain. They allow emotions to ruin their jobs and career. Don't skip from job to job just because you don't like a person. Find more mature solutions, like talking about and airing your differences or asking your manager to mediate. Maturity deals with an issue so it doesn't fester. Immaturity, on the other hand, will cause you a lot of unnecessary pain and drama, causing some of us to stay stuck in low paying jobs.

In this chapter, we saw the power of consistent action to make you a successful person. The last part of the book coming up will tackle the practical questions of how to manage the small amount of money that you may have.

THE GOLDEN NUGGETS

1. As you are at the starting point of a job, you will not get promotions and success straight away, but with patience and consistency, you will get results.

2. 10,000 hours has been proven to be the requirement for one to become world class at what they do. Spend that amount time in your field of expertise.

3. The process of becoming rich and become a success is more important than the riches.

4. To build momentum, you must act with consistency. This will be what brings the massive results in your work endeavours.

RICK MATSOKOTERE

PART 4 – ON MONEY

"Your net worth to the world is usually determined by what remains after your bad habits are subtracted from your good ones."

Ben Franklin

CHAPTER 8 – STOP WORKING FOR THE QUEEN

In the preceding part of the book, we saw how time is the free, yet crucial, resource that is at your disposal to get to greatness in life. In this chapter, I will show how a job and salary are designed to get you to work for the system and not for yourself.

Without knowing how to use money, all our efforts at low wage jobs are futile. Ignorance about money is the reason why people stay broke. It is why you are still suffering even when you get a bit more money.

The system we live in can enslave you if you are not aware of what's happening. After all, the economic system needs worker bees to make it work properly. This doesn't have to be you, though. When I say, "Stop working for the Queen!", I am simply using our monarch as a representation of the government. I am personally a big fan of Her Majesty. Hey Liz, if you're reading this, let's get some tea one of these days. I'm available Fridays!!

Every government system seeks to propagate itself and keep itself in power. If you follow its dictates on how to make use of your money without thinking it through, the government will try to funnel all your money toward itself, rather than help you out. The system is not designed to make you rich or even well off in real terms. Instead, the economic system we live in is designed to take your money.

SLAVERY HIDDEN IN EVERYDAY LIFE

There is a form of slavery hidden in modern day life. I believe modern day slavery is not in chains, but in debt! And it affects people on a low wage more than most. Unfortunately, the slavery is voluntary because even though you get paid a pittance of a salary, the money you get paid, there are people waiting to get that money from you. Every corporation around is trying to take your money, and this means you have to be at work every day just to keep up. As soon as you are paid, you have to pay taxes on everything and insurance for everything, national insurance, utility bills, rent and so forth.

The totality of modern day life is designed to take your money off you as soon as they give your wages. If you are not careful, you could find yourself spending over half of your salary just on payments. Their preferred method is direct debit so that it comes out without you having a chance to think deeply about it.

Then there are those that will lend you money so that you can pay them back with interest. Debt is a sneaky way to get into your pocket and the sneakiest, I find, is consumer debt. It is truly sad that debt is most popular among us low wage workers. Billionaires and people who understand wealth only get into the kind of debt that makes them money, the kind that they want and the kind that they can leverage. On the other hand, we have consumer debt, student debt, mortgages and generally debt that is very difficult to get rid of. Why is it this way? Could it be that rich people know something that we don't?

WHAT ARE YOU WORKING FOR?

There is a vicious cycle of consumerism that threatens to take as much of your money as you allow it to. Many of us live in a vicious cycle of financial survival. It can seem as if the money you get paid each month lasts just long enough to get to the next pay day and that's about it. This, however, is a deliberate state of affairs with architects behind it.

Buying and consuming have become our masters and we have become their slaves. The result, then, is that you end up simply working to pay off stuff that you bought. You go to work, get paid, pay for things that you already bought on credit, then go shopping again in order to find new stuff to buy. You inadvertently find things you cannot afford again and so you put them on yet another payment plan. Even if you get a pay rise at work after working your socks off, immediately you go and increase your spending.

.

Ade's life is an example of this slavery to a salary and a job. He works as a service desk support guy at a major mobile phone operator based in London, and this is what his life every month looks like:

Ade and his wife have a mortgage on their apartment, which is their biggest monthly outgoing. This is a 30-year plan and has them occupied for the foreseeable future. Their next biggest expenses are household bills and travel costs for getting to work each day as well as getting around during evenings and weekends. If these were the only things that they spent their money on, however, life would be simpler. This is not the case.

Life in London is fast-paced and glittery, with adverts left right and centre, showing the young couple what they need to have in order to be seen as successful. Ade has firsthand access to the latest gadgetry coming from the leading technology companies and to help him part with his cash, the company he works for offers him staff discounts. He and his wife get new smart phones annually on the biggest data bundles because they get 25% off. They also have a tablet device each as well as laptops all on these deals.

Ade reckons that the £200 a month he pays for their lives to have the latest TV, internet, mobile and laptop deals is a bargain, that he does not recognise the fact that he is now beholden to his employer to keep working for them so he can continue to enjoy technology at this perceived discount. He works for the system now. He works for his company in terms of being employed by them, but he also works for them by blindly given them and other corporations a large chunk of his salary by direct debit every month!

Ade's story makes us uncomfortable because it resonates too closely with many of us. How much do you pay to your company's cafeteria or coffee kiosk every day? How much do you reinvest in your company in share save schemes every month? Did you know that the investors of your company possibly own shares in the manufacturer of your car, the airline you use to go on holiday, the supermarket chain you use and even the entertainment you consume on the weekend? You are the one who feeds into their system because you do not see how it is important to own, not just to consume. You can change this, though, if you take up my challenge to be more observant about how you interact with the little money you receive every month.

THE MYTH OF BEING TAKEN CARE OF

Do you think I am pointing out conspiracy theories with all this? Seth Godin in his book, Linchpin, talks about something called the "take care of you" bargain. All through the beginning of the boom of corporatism, companies would require their workers to give 50 years of their lives working for them and in return, those companies would promise to take care of the workers and even their families when they retired, got sick or even died. This was a good deal while it lasted. You simply showed up to work and be bodily present and you would get a comfortable lifestyle.

This bargain is not nearly as lucrative today. More and more pensions are failing and governments are letting the people down on their social security obligations. However, we still stake our financial future on them. Why is that? They are not going to take care of you or me. Neither are the big businesses that you spend your hard-earned cash on. The dealer who sold you the BMW that you can barely afford, is never going to pay your bills when you start to struggle.

So why are you paying them an arm and a leg in car finance payments? These companies and government are laying a fine trap for you in order to keep you subservient to them, the rest of your life. The National Health Service in the United Kingdom is creaking at the seams and the government need solutions to avert political disaster. They will not hesitate to use your addiction to consumerism to keep you funding them. If you are not wise in your dealings with tax, spending and taking out credit, then they will squeeze every bit of money out of you and discard you like a used cloth at the end of your life. At that point, they will have their claws deep in your kids.

WHAT YOU DON'T KNOW IS KEEPING YOU POOR

There isn't anything inherently wrong with people who have low paying jobs. We could even prove that the issue is not the small pay you get paid. After all, there are people all over the world who get paid less than you. The men and women who made millions and even billions in the early twentieth century out of meagre subsistence could argue they had much less than you. The thing is, there are principles and secrets that you do not know and these are what are killing you when it comes to money. I would like to speak to you in the rest of this chapter about the things that people with minimum wage jobs, as well as middle class people do not know. These are perceptions we may have on money that are incorrect.

What is it, then, that the rich know that we don't, and should we resent them for it? Obviously, I am not talking about unethical tax dodging schemes, but rich people of a certain level of wealth, usually millionaires, have things they found out about money and they apply those things consistently. Whether it is tax allowances, setting up businesses and offsetting expenses, there are things they know which I, as a budding entrepreneur, don't know. Personally, I decided that instead of being offended by their money, I would find out some of those secrets they knew to wealth creation. Why does the net worth of Bill Gates, Warren Buffett and Jeff Bezos keep going up even in recessions while our money goes the opposite direction?

Question 2: Do you have any money at the end of the month? Money should be retained.

In this chapter, we explored the ways in which an ordinary job is positioned to keep you chained to enriching the system in which you live. Next chapter, we will explore the simple laws of money that are designed to break this cycle of slavery to money by making you a master of your money.

THE GOLDEN NUGGETS

1. The modern-day system of working a job for a salary is the new type of slavery. We are all slaves of those who rule our nations.
2. The cycle of consumerism means most people are mainly working in order to sustain the world economy. All their money leaves them soon after pay day.
3. Employers used to take care of employees, but this is not the case anymore. Instead, they look after you just enough for you to maintain their company.
4. You are a victim and poor because of what you do not know.

CHAPTER 9 – THE SIMPLE LAWS OF MONEY

Last chapter I posed some questions and gave evidence to make you pause and think about how through work and a salary, you have been hoodwinked into slaving away for a system. In this chapter, I will introduce the laws of money that are designed to break your dependence on money through giving you your power back over it.

People who understand how to control money have laws that they use in order to master money, rather than have money be their reason for living. Living in this way has inadvertently helped these people have more money rather than less.

The laws of money are as follows:

1. Money must be retained.

2. Never obey the dictates of money

3. Money is not to be spent, it is to be saved (for investment).

4. Don't spend money on what you can do without.

5. Don't eat tomorrow's food tomorrow.

In this chapter, we are going to look further into each of these. How are your finances at the end of every month? I have, for most of my life, struggled with the problem of having more month at the end of my money. Many people on a low wage suffer from being a financial victim - that is, always spending more than the money we have - or we are simply survivors who just about stay afloat.

RETAINING MONEY

Money must be retained. That is the first step. It is not a sustainable way of living when your money leaves you like your pockets have holes. In order to retain money, the answer isn't winning the lottery, swapping salaries with your boss or having your taxes lowered, no matter how good that may sound. The answer, which even people with a small amount of money can practice, is keeping your expenses at bay.

If you were to be honest with yourself, how much do you have at the end of each month? If you have any money left during that last week before payday, what do you do with it? Do you mysteriously find ways to spend that money? Or can you just look at it and not react? If you master retaining money, as the rich among us have done, then you will be able to use it as a tool to create more through investing.

There are people who are able to, with not much money to start with, invest their money so that it works for them. This way they have gotten out of the rat race, which means that their job is no longer their primary source of income. However, if you never learn how to control your spending and expenses, you will not have anything to invest in the first place.

SPENDING MONEY WE DON'T HAVE, TO BUY THINGS WE DON'T NEED, TO PLEASE PEOPLE WHO DON'T CARE

Trying to keep up with the Joneses is a destructive habit if you have little money to begin with. Buying stuff to impress your neighbours, to uphold cultural norms and to follow trends will end with you going broke or never having any money. Do you really need a Starbucks every day? Can you not make your own coffee instead? There are lots of gourmet coffee brands that can be made at home for a fraction of the price. The perceived loss of status that you may fear is nothing compared to the pain you will go through as a consequence of poor financial decisions. Trust me, I have experienced it firsthand. Retaining money is a good habit to build for your children and your future.

How, then, do you keep your expenses at bay? The first step is to have a proper conversation with the people who matter to you about how much you are spending. Physically write down everything that you spend money on, and start crossing out those things that you don't need. If your situation is bad, and don't kid yourself, it is bad for most people, then be ruthless and say, this £7 I'm spending on lunch on a daily basis can be changed. That £15 haircut you get every week, can it be adjusted in any way? Perhaps getting it every 3 weeks instead? It's all about REDUCE, REDUCE, REDUCE for those expenses.

Do your children go to that fancy private school because of your ego? Is it so you can impress the other parents in your neighbourhood? If it is then you are doing your children a disservice. It would be far better for them to be in an environment that fits their specific needs and that is not measured by the yearly fees.

DON'T EAT TOMORROW'S FOOD TODAY

This law of money is more long term than the others. It speaks to the human tendency to want things immediately if we can't afford them. We buy them now and then pay later. Maybe you see a large screen tv in Costco and buy it to be paid over the next year. Committing to this, however, means giving and selling off your time to the vendor. In a year, there will be another TV that you fancy. This is the simple way of innovation. A better way, by far, is to live by a mantra of not buying if you cannot afford something.

The game of spending today and paying tomorrow is not in your favour. Do you really need to drive that near brand new car today, putting it on finance and paying for it over the next 3 years? In essence, you are forfeiting a part of your salary that hasn't even received yet, to satisfy a craving right now! Moreover In 3 years, the car would have depreciated in a major way. What you have done there is taken the next 3 years of your life and put it on a platter to the car dealer.

What's wrong with living your life in debt, you may ask? It's bad and wrong because you are selling off not only yours, but your children's future with these actions. Instead of leaving them an inheritance, which a responsible parent must do, we are going to leave them debt. This is why I have controversial views on mortgages.

The conventional wisdom is to "get on the property ladder" by buying a house. Do you really understand, however, what a mortgage is? It is a fancy word for a really big debt. The reason the banks want us to call it a mortgage rather a massive debt is because we may think twice before taking one out. What you are doing when you get a mortgage, is selling off 25-30 years of your life to the bank. Literally mortgaging a large part of your life! You cannot quit your job during this time because they will take their house back. You cannot take a sabbatical, travel or do mission or charity work. The house isn't even really yours if you think about it. Try and default on your payments and you will find out pretty quickly who really owns that house.

We are the first generation where our children are worse off financially than their parents. What happened to the selfless nature of parents before who believed intrinsically in making things better for their children? We all just want to live for today as if there will be no tomorrow.

Don't get me wrong. I don't think renting indefinitely is the solution, in fact, I believe those people who will come up with innovative solutions to the real estate and housing market issues will make a killing. When you have a mortgage, however, you don't own the house outright but you have responsibility for all the liabilities connected to it. If it floods, you're responsible for fixing it. If the boiler breaks down, it's on you.

These are all the reasons for which you must master money. Have you noticed that for us low wage workers with the least amount of money, it stays on our mind the longest? When you wake up in the morning and the only reason you have for getting out of bed is your meagre salary, then you are not living a great life. It is a tough and hard one. You end up obeying the dictates of money, sacrificing your family, your dignity and your very life in order to make a little more of it. However, when you learn all the laws of money and habitually, practice them, then money just becomes pieces of paper or numbers on a screen that are tools to accomplish your life purpose.

To conclude this last chapter, I proposed simple practical laws of money that are designed to help you master money from the base level of income you are on right now. Applying them as soon as possible is one of the best things you could do towards going for financial independence.

THE GOLDEN NUGGETS

1. Understanding how the laws of money work will help you go from a financial victim to being in control.
2. Money must be retained. This is the basis of sound financial management.
3. A good rule of thumb is not to spend money you don't have yet and not to live beyond your current station.
4. Credit is a way that companies get you to buy what you desire now and then spend your future paying back. This is not the way to live.

CONCLUSION

Billions of people in the world workforce do jobs that they consider below their skill set or paying under the level they need. Due to this state of dissatisfaction, we can find ourselves resigned to the perceived reality that our jobs are nothing special and just a daily activity to be tolerated.

This book has been written to show you that this is far from the truth and you can change things if you tweak how you story tell to yourself. If you earnestly apply what I presented, you will be happier in what you do for a living and you will convert it into a stepping stone to better success.

I ask that you do one more thing for me if you found value in this book. Give it to a friend, a family member or colleague who needs to read it too. Recommend it to your Facebook, Instagram or LinkedIn pals and we can revolutionise the world of work starting now. Give the book as a gift to the people you are in charge of who may benefit from it; they will thank you for it!

ABOUT THE AUTHOR

Rick Matsokotere has been a student of personal development for over 20 years, putting principles and concepts to the test in the field all throughout his career.

Having done many jobs in the retail, service and IT sectors, Rick climbed the career ladder all the way from McDonalds until he was a analyst with a major energy company in the UK. In 7 years, Rick quadrupled his minimum wage salary working full time and without the advantage of a university degree.

Now, Rick writes, teaches and trains people who want to advance or change their careers through books, online media and tailored talks. He has helped his clients find higher paying jobs, engineer more fulfilling careers, pinpoint their strongest qualities to highlight in interview and performance review situations, and even monetise their hobbies.

Rick lives in Derby where he works as an editor and ghost writer for entrepreneurs and personal development coaches. He also happens to be the biggest Kanye West fan in the world.

Find out more about Rick on his Facebook page: Rick Matsokotere